A Wise Heart

VONETTE
Zachary
BRIGHT

NewLife
PUBLICATIONS

My Heart in His Hands Bible Study: A Wise Heart
Published by
NewLife Publications
A ministry of Campus Crusade for Christ
P.O. Box 620877
Orlando, FL 32862-0877

ISBN 1-56399-180-2

Design and production by Genesis Group

Cover design by Koechel Peterson & Associates, Inc., Minneapolis, MN

Printed in the United States of America

Unless otherwise indicated, Scripture quotations are from the *New International Version*, © 1973, 1978, 1984 by the International Bible Society. Published by Zondervan Bible Publishers, Grand Rapids, Michigan.

For more information, write:
L.I.F.E., Campus Crusade for Christ—P.O. Box 40, Flemington Markets, 2129, Australia
Campus Crusade for Christ of Canada—Box 529, Sumas, WA 98295
Campus Crusade for Christ—Fairgate House, King's Road, Tyseley, Birmingham, B11 2AA, United Kingdom
Lay Institute for Evangelism, Campus Crusade for Christ—P.O. Box 8786, Auckland, 1035, New Zealand
Campus Crusade for Christ—9 Lock Road #3-03, PacCan Centre, Singapore
Great Commission Movement of Nigeria—P.O. Box 500, Jos, Plateau State, Nigeria, West Africa
Campus Crusade for Christ International—100 Lake Hart Drive, Orlando, FL 32832, USA

Contents

My Dear Friends

I want to welcome you to this Bible study series for women! I'm excited about the opportunity to walk through the Scriptures with you as we explore all that God's Word has for the busy woman of today.

Every unique detail of a woman's life fits into a grand and glorious plan. My prayer is that women of all ages will desire to have a deeper relationship with God, and to discover the joys of knowing Him and His plan for their lives.

God's Word speaks so directly to every aspect of a woman's life. It fills us with wisdom, imparts God's love, and provides ample instructions for our daily walk. The Scriptures tell us the results we can expect when we live in agreement with God's plan, and what we can expect if we do not live as He directs.

The Bible has much to say about its value and relevance for our lives today. It gives us guidance: "Your word is a lamp to my feet and a light for my path" (Psalm 119:105). It gives understanding: "The unfolding of your words gives light; it gives understanding to the simple" (Psalm 119:130). It is not made up of cold, dead words, but living, Spirit-filled words that can affect our hearts and our lives: "For the word of God is living and active. Sharper than any double-edged sword, it penetrates even to dividing soul and spirit, joints and marrow; it judges the thoughts and attitudes of the heart" (Hebrews 4:12).

When I wrote the devotional books for the series *My Heart In His Hands*, it was with the desire to encourage women and to help them realize that God is interested and involved in the details of their lives. My goal was to provide a practical and systematic way for a woman to examine her heart and recognize how beautifully God has created her. This set of study guides has been designed to complement each seasonal devotional.

Each study guide has been developed prayerfully and can be used for individual or group study. Perhaps you are part of a group that meets regularly to study and discuss the precious treasures of God's Word. I have been a part of such groups for many years, and I am still overjoyed to meet with these women.

Whether you will study on your own or with others, it is my heartfelt prayer that you will open your heart to His Word and enjoy the blessing of resting confidently in His hands.

From my heart to yours,

Vonette Z. Bright

How to Use This Study

The *My Heart in His Hands* Bible study series is designed for the busy woman who desires a deeper walk with God. The twenty lessons in *A Wise Heart* embrace the glorious truth that God imparts wisdom to those who ask, giving us the tools to live above the fray.

A Wise Heart provides everything you need to understand biblical principles and use them to transform your life. Whether you are working hard at your career, involved in full-time ministry, knee-deep in preschoolers, or raising teenagers, you can find the time to complete the short lessons and receive encouragement for your day. The questions require less time than most courses so that you can fit Bible study into your hectic schedule. The refreshing look at Scripture passages will help you apply God's Word to your daily needs.

You can use this book as an individual study during your quiet time with God, or as a group study with other women. (A Discussion Guide with answers to the Bible questions is located at the back of this book to help a group facilitator.) It can also be used as a companion to the *My Heart in His Hands* devotional series.

The book contains an in-depth look at the lives of two women: a biblical portrait of a godly woman and an inspirational portrait of an outstanding contemporary woman. These portraits, woven throughout the book, give insights into a wise heart.

Each lesson includes these parts:

- His Word—a Scripture passage to read
- Knowing His Heart—understanding God's Word
- Knowing My Heart—personal questions to consider
- My Heart in His Hands—a timely quote to ponder

Whether to start your morning or end your day, you can use this study to focus on God's Word and on His marvelous works in your life. As you apply these principles, you will truly discover a wise heart!

A Wise Heart

So many in our society take advice from Hollywood. A starlet appears on a late-night talk show and gushingly describes her new relationship with a well-known actor. She tells how well their personalities fit together, and declares that this man is her "soul mate." She outlines her ideals for a relationship, which may or may not include marriage, and doles out advice on love.

All across the world, women listen and hang on her every word. They believe her when she says this relationship is "forever." And many apply her relationship advice to their own lives.

Then what happens? Often, after only a year or two of marriage, this starlet is explaining to the press why the relationship didn't work out. "My husband and I just weren't compatible." Their "amicable" divorce may include months of bitter fighting.

Then a few months later, this same woman appears, exclaiming that she and her new love will be together forever. She once again gives her opinion on how to build a strong relationship.

Why do women pattern their lives after people who continue to make the same blunders? Why don't they see what's wrong with the advice proffered by those with questionable values?

You probably have answers for these questions. Most people in our society have lost their moral bearings. They float from one opinion to another, according to how they feel at the moment, how the advice fits in with their own desires, and how well the messenger presents the message. One year, marriage is "outdated" and living together will make one happy. The next year, weddings are back in style, but only with a prenuptial agreement. Who knows which fad will prevail in the future?

The thinking of the world is not wisdom; it is foolishness.

That's what Paul writes in 1 Corinthians 1:20. Only God has the wisdom that can enable us to lead productive, holy, joyful lives. Only His Spirit can protect us from making horrendous mistakes that cost our loved ones and ourselves dearly.

The woman who places her heart in God's hands will be in touch with the wisdom of the ages. God always handles our concerns with tenderness and compassion. His desire is for us to live in His love and support. We have no fear when we rely on Him to direct our lives and help us make wise choices.

Proverbs wonderfully describes the person who allows God to control her life and family: "By wisdom a house is built, and through understanding it is established; through knowledge its rooms are filled with rare and beautiful treasures" (24:3,4). King David writes, "Surely I was sinful at birth, sinful from the time my mother conceived me. Surely you desire truth in the inner parts; you teach me wisdom in the inmost place" (Psalm 51:5,6). Because of our sinful nature, we cannot act wisely. But as children of God, we can be filled with His wisdom. He gave us His Son as an example so we can make wise choices. He also gave us His Spirit so we can partake of His power and strength.

The breadth of God's wisdom is beyond our understanding. But He gives us what we need to live according to His will and His ways. These lessons will give you the hope and the practical steps to apply God's wisdom to your life. Part 1 shows our need for wisdom, while Part 2 brings us to the Source of wisdom, our eternal God. Part 3 delves into the nuts and bolts of wisdom, and Part 4 provides ways we can tap into the Source of wisdom.

I encourage you to study these lessons with a deep commitment to apply God's Word to the day-to-day choices in your life. The principles you learn can be used in your marriage, in relating to your children or grandchildren, in your ministry, or in your chosen profession. God is waiting to help you live above the worldly "wisdom" that leads to foolishness.

The Heart of Deborah

O ver the last few decades, my heart has been broken over the moral decline in our wonderful country. My deepest sorrow is over the pain we cause our God when we drift away from Him and His laws. At the same time, my heart goes out to the millions of people who are suffering: the children struggling in drug-infested and abusive homes, the family members devastated by broken marriages, the fearful victims of violent crime.

Thousands of years ago, Deborah lived in a similar time of distress. She was a judge during a period in Israel's history when the people were caught up in idolatry and immorality. What must it have been like for her to hear cases involving sinful acts and ungodly attitudes? She must have been greatly concerned for her people. Surely, Deborah realized that God would deal with the nation's sins.

And He did. To punish the Israelites, God gave them over to the rule of Jabin, the king of Canaan. The Israelites were cruelly oppressed for twenty years.

During this time, Deborah, a prophetess, was leading Israel. As judge, she held court under a palm tree where she settled the disputes of the Israelites.

Judges not only handled civil concerns, but were military deliverers. One day, after the Lord spoke to Deborah, she called for Barak and told him: "The Lord, the God of Israel, commands you: 'Go, take with you ten thousand men of Naphtali and Zebulun and lead the way to Mount Tabor. I will lure Sisera, the commander of Jabin's army, with his chariots and his troops to the Kishon River and give him into your hands'" (Judges 4:6,7).

In recent years, a debate has been raging about the role of women in the U.S. military. Should they fight on the front lines? Should they serve in confined quarters such as submarines? But no one debated Deborah's role in war. Instead, Barak begged her to accompany him. In fact, he was willing to go only if Deborah went with him. Deborah agreed to go, but she prophesied that because of his unwillingness to take the leadership, the honor for Sisera's defeat would go to a woman. Still, Barak wanted her presence. Her counsel was that valuable.

When Sisera found out that Barak and an army of men had gone up to Mount Tabor, he took 900 chariots and all his men to the Kishon River. Deborah went to Barak and said, "Go! This is the day the LORD has given Sisera into your hands."

Barak followed Deborah's counsel and Sisera's army was defeated that day. Sisera fled on foot. He found shelter in the tent of Jael, the wife of Heber the Kenite, someone he thought would be sympathetic to his plight. Jael invited him in, gave him some milk, and covered him with a blanket. As he lay sleeping, she picked up a tent peg and hammer and drove the peg through his temple, killing him.

When Barak came by, Jael showed him the commander's body. As Deborah had predicted, a woman had received the honor of defeating Sisera! And the Israelites enjoyed a time of peace.

God had blessed Deborah with the gift of prophecy, and she had used her gift wisely. She did not squander it on selfish or frivolous endeavors. Instead, she willingly served wherever God needed her. Deborah was a woman with a heart for God.

The Heart of Henrietta Mears

Big hats, little hats. Bold hats, sophisticated hats. Blue hats, purple hats, yellow hats, pink hats. Hats of every shape and size. Henrietta Mears loved wearing hats. It was her trademark, and she collected them on her travels around the world. Everyone who knew her knew she loved hats.

Miss Mears' life was as colorful as her hat collection. She was born in 1890 in Fargo, North Dakota. At 7 years old, she announced that she was ready to become a Christian. Her mother was cautious at first because of her young age, but a few weeks later, Henrietta presented herself to the congregation. She clearly and frankly answered questions about her faith and doctrine. How many of us could do the same even now?

As a teenager, Henrietta committed her life to service for God, although she felt no specific call to a certain area. After graduating from college, Henrietta taught school in Minnesota. She and her sister, Margaret, made their home together. Over the years, Margaret's homemaking talents allowed Henrietta the freedom to work and minister to many people.

One Sunday, Dr. Stewart P. MacLennan, pastor of First Presbyterian Church of Hollywood, California, preached in the church Miss Mears attended. She was moved by his message, but did not know that this meeting would change her life forever.

Searching for God's will on the direction of her life, Miss Mears took a one-year sabbatical from teaching. She and Margaret traveled through Europe and then went to California. While there, they visited Dr. MacLennan's church. He was impressed with Miss Mears and asked her to join his staff as Director of Christian Education.

She struggled with this decision. Should she leave her teaching? Could she and Margaret sell their house? Could she leave her friends? "Throwing down the fleece," Miss Mears raised the asking price for the house by $2,000. If someone would pay that much, she would have God's answer. To her amazement, someone did offer the full amount, and in 1928 she and Margaret began their new lives in California.

Miss Mears had a clear purpose for her ministry. She once said, "Don't try to build a bigger Sunday school. Don't have a visitation campaign to get more people. Build a *better* Sunday school. Have a place for every person, every age." Her ideas were ahead of her time. She created graded programs for every age. She introduced worship services before class, expanded the educational facilities, and attracted young people by offering a program to meet their interests and ambitions.

She believed God deserved the best we have to give to Him. When she found the Sunday school material sorely lacking, she wrote page after page of lessons, which were then typed, stapled, and put into books for the church's use. By 1933, she created Gospel Light Press, publishing twelve full courses that year.

Miss Mears also discipled young leaders within the church, including Billy Graham, Bill Bright, and Richard Halverson, former U.S. Senate chaplain. Her missionary heart birthed GLINT (Gospel Literature International), which provides quality Bible study materials to poor, unchurched nations.

Henrietta Mears was a remarkable woman, not because of her own talents and abilities, but because she allowed God to guide her. He multiplied her gifts and used them to affect lives around the world. Her life is an example of godly wisdom.

PART 1

Wisdom Is a Choice

Any woman who has had the privilege of parenting teenagers knows that it takes a lot of wisdom. How can anyone find wisdom to cope with seemingly endless crises in the life of a high school student?

One mother was caught off guard when her bubbly daughter bounded in from school. "Guess what!" she exclaimed. "One of my friends is going to have a baby!"

"Oh, no," the mother gasped. "She's still in high school! She's too young."

But "young" wasn't the way her daughter would describe herself or her friends. They were practically grown up. "My friend is going to keep her baby," the girl informed her mother proudly.

"She'll be a good mother."

"She doesn't have the maturity or skills to be a mother," the woman explained. "That will be so devastating for the baby! And for your friend!"

But those arguments made little sense to the daughter. She was so excited about the idea of a brand new baby that she couldn't sort out the moral, emotional, and spiritual problems in her friend's situation.

The mother didn't know how to help her daughter see the fallacies of the choices her friend had made. So she just quietly kept on teaching her daughter, pointing out what God says and the consequences for disobeying His established order for families. She also realized that her teen was not able to make wise choices in this area, so she adjusted her rules accordingly.

Months later, the daughter came to her and admitted, "Mom, you were right. Being a mother is more than having a baby." Then the two of them were able to discuss in depth the importance of abstinence before marriage.

All around us—in our neighborhoods, at our workplaces, at the gym, and even in our own lives—we can see the disastrous results of making unwise choices. The world is certainly no place to go to find answers! Every area of our society is reeling from the effects of people who act heedlessly or are following bad advice.

Wisdom comes from God and our greatest resource is the Bible. Without it, we are merely going down a road with no map and will end up in a mire that will cause us indescribable pain. But like that teenager, we may feel sure we are headed in the right direction even when disaster lays just over the next hill.

God will not only help us make the right choices, He will also reveal the wondrous plans He has for our lives as we obey Him. In His wisdom, we can be all He intends us to be!

I Want to Be Wise

What do you want to be when you grow up?" You've probably asked that question many times of children, teenagers, and young adults. I'm sure their answers have varied widely—a fireman or policeman, a parent or teacher, an animal trainer or biologist. Each of us wants to *do* something important when we grow up. But as we get older and learn what is truly important in life, our focus changes from what we *do* to who we *are*. Suddenly, our career is just a job. Our profession is not our life's work, but our *life* becomes our life's work. If someone were to ask you today, "What do you want to be when you grow up?" what would your answer be? Perhaps it might be, "I want to be wise." The Book of James gives us practical principles that will help us grow to be more godly in our wisdom.

His **WORD**: James 3:13–18

KNOWING *His* **HEART**

1. According to verse 13, how is wisdom demonstrated?

2. What does verse 14 tell us to do with "bitter envy" and "self-ish ambition"?

3. Verses 15 and 16 speak of wisdom that is not from heaven. How do these verses describe it?

4. In contrast, how do verses 17 and 18 describe heavenly wisdom?

KNOWING *My* HEART

1. How has your life recently demonstrated "deeds done in the humility that comes from wisdom"?

2. What evidence have you found in your life of bitter envy or selfish ambition?

3. How are the evidences of wisdom given in verse 17 reflected in your life?

4. How would your life be different if you were to "sow in peace"?

My HEART IN *His* HANDS

"*Seeing the Lord only giveth wisdom, let every one seriously set himself by prayer in secret to seek it of him (Prov. 2,3).*"
—HARVARD UNIVERSITY RULES AND PRECEPTS, 1642

I Want to Make Wise Choices

Our lives are full of decisions—big ones and little ones. We are faced with choices every day and sometimes we don't know which way to go. Should we or shouldn't we? Turn to the left or to the right? Move or stay? Follow God's will or our own? Although the big decisions can greatly affect the course of our lives, the "little" decisions demonstrate who we are and who we are following. Because we don't know when a seemingly inconsequential decision will turn out to be a life-changing one, it's important to always choose wisely. God's wisdom allows us to make a lifetime of good decisions. This lesson looks at choices made by the ten virgins in the parable in Matthew 25.

His **WORD:** Matthew 25:1–13

KNOWING *His* **HEART**

1. What did the wise virgins do differently from the foolish virgins in verses 3 and 4?

2. What did both sets of virgins do when they heard that the bridegroom was coming?

3. What was the result of the wise virgins being prepared?

4. How did the bridegroom respond to the foolish virgins when they came to the door?

KNOWING *My* HEART

1. What part can unpreparedness play in unwise decisions?

2. Think of a time when you made an unwise decision. What were the consequences?

3. How can you avoid making the same kind of unwise choice in the future?

4. If the Bridegroom (Jesus) were coming back tomorrow, what do you need to do today to get ready for Him?

My HEART IN *His* HANDS

"Ask God for wisdom, courage, and continuing direction to live against the flow when the flow is not with the God of Wisdom."
—SANDRA DRESCHER-LEHMAN

Wisdom Can Be Shared

Family traditions are a wonderful way to stay connected with generations past. Spring vacations. Summer picnics. Thanksgiving dinner. Christmas morning. Each day, each season, each holiday brings events and activities that are repeated and passed down. These traditions can be a source of stability in an ever-changing world, and transmit to the next generation a sense of what is important. But over time, even the most entrenched traditions may change to meet the needs of the current generation. But there is one tradition that should never change—the passing of faith in the God of our fathers and the wisdom that comes from God. Each generation has a responsibility to share the blessings that God has generously given. In Proverbs 22, we will see wisdom shared as God intends.

His **WORD:** Proverbs 22:17–21

KNOWING *His* **HEART**

1. According to verses 17 and 18, what are we to do with the "sayings of the wise"?

2. Why should we learn from the wise ones (verse 19)?

3. How does Solomon, who wrote most of the Book of Proverbs, describe the "sayings" he has given us (verses 20 and 21)?

4. How should we respond to the wise words we have been given?

KNOWING *My* HEART

1. Who in your life would you consider to be a wise person? What qualities does this person have that make her wise?

2. Give examples of how the wisdom of other people has been important in your life.

3. In what ways can you impart to others the wisdom you have acquired?

4. For which areas of your life do you currently need wisdom?

My HEART IN *His* HANDS

"The influence of a holy woman cannot be measured."

—JOY DAWSON

The Rain Will Come

Rain is a blessing. It supplies moisture for our crops, provides water for life, and even powers our cities. But there are times when it can seem like a curse. It can cause damaging floods or make outdoor work miserable. Yet, whether a blessing or curse, it is God who orchestrates the rain. Matthew 5:45 says, "He causes his sun to rise on the evil and the good, and sends rain on the righteous and the unrighteous." God sends rain to all people for their benefit, even if it doesn't seem like a benefit at the time. We will each have days of sunshine and happiness, and we will have days of rain and testing. Yet knowing that God is in control of both the sun and the rain is a source of great comfort. The wisdom that we receive from God will help us in times of sunshine, but more importantly, in times of rain.

His **WORD:** Matthew 7:24–27

KNOWING *His* **HEART**

1. What is the comparison being made in verse 24?

2. What happens to the man's house in verse 25?

3. How is the foolish man described in verse 26?

4. What inevitably happened to the foolish man's house?

KNOWING *My* HEART

1. When was the last time you faced "rain and wind"? How did applying or not applying the Word of God affect your response to this trial?

2. In what ways have you been like the foolish builder?

3. How can following God's direction make you a wiser builder?

4. How will knowing that God is in the "rain" as well as the "sunshine" help you face both good times and difficult ones?

My HEART IN *His* HANDS

"A house will not stand without a foundation. And we need a very firm foundation to stand against the onslaught of the forces around us. We need Jesus Christ."

—CAROLE MAYHALL

LESSON 5

God Has Big Plans

When problems arise, people seek out those who have proved helpful in the past. Both Deborah and Henrietta Mears found themselves in positions where they were influential in the lives of others. They had accepted responsibilities that caused others to look up to them. Because the women chose to follow God's wisdom, He expanded their areas of influence. This is true for any woman. We learn wisdom by taking small steps that lead to bigger ones. If we are faithful to put God first in a crisis, He will bring hurting people our way who need the same answers to their problems. If we faithfully attend a women's Bible study group, we may be asked to lead one. If we seek God's face during a personal difficulty, we will be able to give answers and comfort others. God can use the woman with a wise heart!

His **WORD:** Judges 4: 1–7

KNOWING *His* **HEART**

1. What was Israel's situation as Deborah's story began?

2. Why did the people look to Deborah for help?

3. How did God guide Henrietta Mears as she sought His will for her life?

4. In what ways did Miss Mears share God's wisdom with those to whom she ministered?

KNOWING *My* HEART

1. When your faith was tested and you faced uncertainties like the Israelites, how did God's Word help you gain wisdom?

2. When people look to you for advice or counsel, how do you respond?

3. Why is it important to seek God's counsel in decision-making?

4. How can you help others to know God's wisdom?

My HEART IN *His* HANDS

"Christ taught that a man finds his true self only when he is willing to lose himself in God's plan."

—HENRIETTA MEARS

PART 2

Wisdom Leads Us to God

Have you ever received an anonymous gift? Perhaps you opened a package at Christmas time and found something that just suited your taste. What a wonderful feeling! But then you may have felt an intense desire to know who the thoughtful person was. A close friend? A favorite relative? A kind neighbor? If you are like many women, you won't rest until you discover the identity of that special gift-giver.

Many times we receive the gift of wisdom, but do we know who gave it to us? Wisdom is such an important part of our lives. It affects every nook and cranny of our existence. Sometimes we make wise choices without even realizing where the wisdom originated. Other times we make poor choices because we don't consult the Source of our wisdom.

Job questioned where wisdom was hiding. "Where can wisdom be found? Where does understanding dwell? Man does not comprehend its worth; it cannot be found in the land of the living" (Job 28:12,13). Then Job considered many parts of creation and destruction and death but could not find wisdom in any of them.

Eventually, Job concludes, "God understands the way to it and he alone knows where it dwells, for he views the ends of the earth and sees everything under the heavens . . . And he said to man, 'The fear of the Lord—that is wisdom, and to shun evil is understanding'" (Job 28:23,24,28).

Throughout the Old and New Testaments, true wisdom is ascribed to God alone. Yet He imparts wisdom to us, as we can see from Psalm 25:14: "The LORD confides in those who fear him; he makes his covenant known to them." In Ecclesiastes we read, "To the man who pleases him, God gives wisdom, knowledge and happiness" (2:26).

Have you experienced this truth in your own life? God's wisdom comes in many forms we don't usually consider. Conviction of sin is the Holy Spirit's way of showing us what we are doing wrong and how to correct our ways. Through conviction and repentance, we are spared many devastating consequences. Allowing trials to come into our life is another way God shares His wisdom with us. Through hard times, we seek His face more earnestly, and we find wisdom and learn truths that the good times could never teach us.

When we seek the Source of all wisdom, we will discover qualities in God's nature that compliment His wisdom. These lessons will help assure us that God is able and willing to give us all we need to live a life that is pleasing to Him.

LESSON 6

God, the All-Powerful

The salt-water crocodile is the largest reptile in the world. A fully grown adult male can reach 20 feet in length and weigh more than a ton. Its very strong jaws are used to kill large mammals such as cattle, deer, and buffalo. These reptiles are fierce and powerful members of the animal kingdom. Although most people would not find them the least bit attractive, their power and strength are awe-inspiring. Yet as powerful as the crocodile is, it is still just a creation of Almighty God, wielding its power by instinct. The God we serve is infinitely more powerful, and His power and strength should be infinitely more awe-inspiring for us, His children. His power is executed in wisdom. In the Book of Daniel, we will discover many ways that God is powerful and see the many reasons that we should praise Him.

His **WORD:** Daniel 2:19–23

KNOWING *His* **HEART**

1. What two things mentioned in verse 20 belong to God alone?

2. From verse 21, what actions does God take with His wisdom?

3. Which actions demonstrate God's power?

4. What does God's wisdom enable Him to do (verse 22)?

KNOWING *My* HEART

1. Describe an incident in your life where God has shown His power. What specific wisdom was revealed?

2. What is the importance of wisdom and discernment?

3. How does it impact your life to know that God reveals what is deep and hidden and knows what lies in darkness?

4. For what aspects of God's wisdom and power can you thank and praise Him right now?

My HEART IN *His* HANDS

"The sum total of all the power in all the universe would be like a toenail on the person of God."

—TONY EVANS

LESSON 7

Jesus, Our Wisdom

If you are like most people, you probably have questions that you would like answered, such as: Why do Christians suffer? Why are there wars and famine? How does God work through pain and suffering? Why did Jesus come as an infant and preach about servanthood? You might wonder if God will ever reveal the answers. Rest assured that He will—in fact, He already has. All the answers have been revealed through our Lord and Savior, Jesus Christ. As you get to know Him better, you will discover more and more answers. First Corinthians 1:30 tells us, "Christ Jesus...has become for us wisdom from God." It is through Christ that we will know and understand the challenges and mysteries of life that we face.

His **WORD:** 1 Corinthians 1:26–31

KNOWING *His* HEART

1. How does verse 26 describe Christians before God called them?

2. In verses 27–29, how did God redeem these qualities?

3. According to verse 30, from where does wisdom come?

4. Why should we boast in the Lord and not in ourselves?

KNOWING *My* HEART

1. In what ways was your thinking different before you accepted Christ as your Savior?

2. How has God worked through your weaknesses to achieve His purposes?

3. What can you boast about in your life that has come from Christ's Spirit living in you?

4. How can the wisdom of Christ help you with a specific decision you are facing?

My HEART IN *His* HANDS

"In [Christ] we have set before us. . . a model of feeling and action, adapted to all times, places, and circumstances; and combining so much of wisdom, benevolence, and holiness, that none can fathom its sublimity; and yet, presented in a form so simple, that even a child may be made to understand and taught to love it."

—BENJAMIN FRANKLIN BUTLER
U.S. Attorney General, 1833-1838

LESSON 8

God, Our Creator

Scientists estimate that there may be as many as 100 million species of living organisms on earth. Only 1.75 million have been identified. Yet God uniquely equipped each to function in a world filled with other creatures. Let's look at just one type of creature. Have you ever tried to identify all the birds you see? Each species is a different shape, size, and color. On a beautiful spring morning, the many different chirps, calls, and whistles sound like a chorus from heaven. God made each type of bird unique and gave them a language to communicate with each other. Amazingly, He has given each species unique characteristics to both distinguish it and enable it to survive. Our God has taken great care to create an ecosystem that functions cooperatively and intricately. He took the same care when He created His most special creation, humans. As we look at the words of Job, we will see how all of creation owes everything to God.

His WORD: Job 9: 4–10

KNOWING *His* HEART

1. How does verse 4 describe God?

2. How is the creation affected by God's wrath (verses 5–7)?

3. What do verses 8 and 9 tell us of God as the Creator?

4. How does God's creative power relate to human needs (verse 10)?

KNOWING *My* HEART

1. What does it mean to you to know about God's profound wisdom and vast power?

2. What can you look to in the natural world that shows the wisdom of God, the Creator?

3. Do you consider yourself wiser now than you were 10 years ago? How specifically has God enabled your growth in wisdom?

4. How should you respond to God as the source of all wisdom?

My HEART IN *His* HANDS

"There is but one law for all, namely that law which governs all law, the law of our Creator, the law of humanity, justice, equality."
—EDMUND BURKE

LESSON 9

The Holy Spirit, Our Guide

Something told me not to get on the plane." "I just felt I needed to talk with that stranger." "There was a tug on my heart to go see the woman at the nursing home." How many times have you had seemingly inexplicable urges to do or say something? If these actions result in a blessing to you or someone else, this "voice" is not just your own random thoughts. As a follower of Christ, you are hearing the voice of His Spirit speaking to you. The Holy Spirit dwells within us from the moment we invited Christ into our lives, and He is counseling us daily to make us more like Christ. If you truly seek wisdom, you will endeavor to hear the voice of the Holy Spirit more clearly in all you do. When we ask, He will guide us in the truth.

His **WORD:** 1 Corinthians 2:6–16

KNOWING *His* **HEART**

1. What kind of wisdom is being spoken of in verse 7?

2. What reasons for hope do we find in verses 9 and 10?

3. What comparison is made in verse 11 between God and man?

4. List the benefits to someone who has the Spirit of God, as given in verses 12–16.

KNOWING *My* HEART

1. How does it affect your decision-making to know that the Spirit who searches "even the deep things of God" inhabits you?

2. Think of the person you know best; have this person's words or actions ever surprised you? How does this apply to God's work in your life?

3. How is the "spiritual man" demonstrated in your life?

4. How has having the "mind of Christ" changed your life? How will it change your future?

My HEART IN *His* HANDS

"If the Christian life is simply a matter of doing our best, there was no need for God to send the Holy Spirit to help us."

—CHARLES STANLEY

LESS⊖N 10

Wisdom's Result, Peace

Judges chapter 5 ends, "Then the land had peace for forty years." This was the result of relying on God's wisdom: peace. For us, peace isn't always freedom from conflict, but is the quietness of spirit we experience from doing things God's way. For example, one who follows biblical wisdom in her finances won't get deeply into debt or spend money on unhealthy practices. She will be better prepared for financial ups and downs and will experience the joy of sacrificial giving to the Lord. By following God's wisdom, Deborah and Henrietta Mears found peace that led to joy. Deborah expressed her joy in a song of praise to God. Miss Mears found the joy of fulfillment—to the end of her life. As she viewed housing going up, she was filled with new ideas on how to reach those people for Christ. Her heart was singing. That night the Lord took her home, into the presence of the One who had inspired her.

His WORD: Judges 5

KNOWING *His* HEART

1. In what ways are praises offered to God (verses 1–3)?

2. What power did God display when the people had followed Him in the past (verses 4 and 5)?

3. Describe the attitudes and actions of the people in verses 9–13.

4. From Miss Mears' example, how does having God's wisdom relate to peace?

KNOWING *My* HEART

1. When Deborah and Henrietta Mears followed the Lord, how were people around them affected?

2. How have you had a similar affect on others in your life as a parent or as a family member?

3. Describe the peace you have experienced as a result of following God in a difficult time of your life.

4. List ways you will praise God for His wisdom.

My HEART IN *His* HANDS

"Lord, teach us true serenity, the blessing of tranquility,
Let us find our deepest joy in Thee—give us peace within your love."

—B. J. HOFF

PART 3

Wisdom Involves Action

King Solomon was the wisest person who ever lived. Yet at times he didn't do the right thing and suffered the consequences. He had many wives and his children didn't follow the Lord. After his death, his son led the nation into idolatry, splitting it into two kingdoms because of his unwise actions.

How could the wisest of men make such huge mistakes? Although Solomon was given wisdom from God, he failed to put it into practice. Instead, he relied on his own "wisdom," which can never measure up. First Corinthians 3:19 says that the wisdom of the world is foolishness to God. We can see many examples of this truth in our society. Greedy men place their wealth in risky investments that fail. Parents follow the leading advice on raising children only to find their family in turmoil. Singles believe that sex before marriage is all right, then they suffer from disease and emotional pain. Paul writes that people who consider themselves wise are really fools (Romans 1:22). And Isaiah tells us that the wisdom of the wisest person will perish and the understanding of the most intelligent will disappear (29:14).

The only wisdom that will last is God's. Romans 11:33 describes His unfathomable nature: "Oh, the depth of the riches of the wisdom and knowledge of God! How unsearchable his judgments, and his paths beyond tracing out!" We will never truly understand God's wisdom because it is so far above us. Solomon calls wisdom precious, of greater value than any kind of wealth (Proverbs 8:11).

If our natural wisdom is foolishness and God's wisdom is beyond our understanding, how can we ever find out what wisdom is? We discover it through the following actions:

1. *Fear the Lord.* Proverbs 9:10 tells us, "The fear of the LORD is the beginning of wisdom." When we fear the Lord, our hearts turn to Him and we partake of His wisdom. Rather than following our own thoughts, which are distorted by worldly influences and our sin nature, we look toward God in humility.

2. *Follow the ways of God.* The prophet Hosea explains: "Who is wise? He will realize these things. Who is discerning? He will understand them. The ways of the LORD are right, the righteous walk in them, but the rebellious stumble in them" (Hosea 14:9). We have two choices: obey God even if we don't understand, or rebel against Him and bring disaster to our lives.

3. *Gain experience.* Elihu tells Job that he thought age would teach wisdom. But then he discovered that years alone do not make a person wise. We have all known people who make the same mistakes repeatedly, causing themselves deeper pain.

In the next five lessons, we will consider different aspects of God's wisdom and how it can be applied to our situations.

LESSON 11

Knowing God's Will

Psychics. Fortunetellers. Astrologers. The world is filled with people who want to tell what the future holds. That's because the world is filled with people who want to know their future. Who will I marry? Where will I live? What will I be doing ten years from now? When will I die? These are all questions to which we want answers. The world's way is to try to foretell these things through many unbiblical methods. While we as Christians would also like to know these things, the primary question is this: What is God's will for my life? God has provided a way for us to know His will to the extent that He wants us to know it. We will look at the Book of Ephesians to see the importance of knowing God's will for our lives.

His WORD: Ephesians 5:15–18

KNOWING *His* HEART

1. What is the caution given to us in verse 15?

2. How does "making the most of every opportunity" in verse 16 relate to the previous verse?

3. What do you think is meant by "the days are evil" (verse 16)?

4. How can we not be foolish (verses 17 and 18)?

KNOWING *My* HEART

1. Why is it important for you to live a life of wisdom?

2. What can you do to make the most of opportunities you are facing right now? In the future?

3. In what ways are "the days evil" in the world around you?

4. How can you apply this passage to determining what the Lord's will is in your life?

My HEART IN *His* HANDS

"I can't imagine having to 'guess' at what I should do. I couldn't bear the loneliness of feeling that I could only talk to myself. The God I'm looking for—and maybe the God you're looking for—is a God who guides us in the everyday activities and interactions of life."

—BILL HYBELS

LESSON 12

Having Discernment

Discernment is "the act or process of exhibiting keen insight and good judgment." Discernment is being able to see the truth of a situation under the surface and making wise choices. Discernment is being able to see the motives behind people's actions. More important than knowing its definition is knowing its source. True discernment comes from God, and is one element of wisdom. God is all-knowing, all-powerful, merciful, and just. He wants to help us with the challenges in our life. Godly discernment helps us know when to speak up and when to keep silent. It helps us to ask the right questions and hear the truth behind the answers. In this lesson, we will see how an ancient king used godly discernment to settle a volatile dispute.

His WORD: 1 Kings 3:16–28

KNOWING *His* HEART

1. When the women went before King Solomon, what was his initial solution (verses 23–25)?

2. How did the women respond to the king's order (verse 26)?

3. Why do you think the king ruled as he did (verse 27)?

4. How did the people view Solomon after his verdict?

KNOWING *My* HEART

1. What conflicts do you face for which you could use wisdom such as Solomon had?

2. How could your life be different if you applied God's wisdom to these conflicts?

3. Have you known someone about whom you could say, "She had the wisdom of Solomon"? What made this person so wise?

4. How does the world respond to people who demonstrate God's wisdom?

My HEART IN *His* HANDS

"There are two kinds of people: those who say to God, 'Thy will be done,' and those to whom God says, 'All right, then, have it your way.'"
—C. S. LEWIS

LESSON 13

Understanding God's Mystery

Sherlock Holmes, Nancy Drew, James Bond—these names remind us of mystery. A crime is committed and clues are left for the great detectives of the world to solve. As they collect evidence, the detectives try to piece together the details of the crime and, ultimately, the criminal's motive. These storybook mysteries nearly always end in resolution, but there are some mysteries that no detective can solve. These are the mysteries of God. He reveals the answers to life's questions as He wants to—giving us only what we need to know. He provides the answers through His Word and through His Son. Like the great detectives of literature, we will see that finding the answers to the mysteries—God's mysteries—will have rich rewards.

His **WORD:** Colossians 1:24–29

KNOWING *His* **HEART**

1. What is the commission God gave to Paul (verses 24 and 25)?

2. How is God's Word described in verse 26?

3. What is the essence or "the glorious riches" of this mystery?

4. According to verse 28, what are believers to do?

KNOWING *My* HEART

1. Describe a circumstance in your life in which God's will seems a mystery.

2. Why do you think Paul rejoiced over His suffering?

3. In what ways have you suffered for Christ or His Church? What was your reaction?

4. How can you put into practice the actions mentioned in verse 28?

My HEART IN *His* HANDS

"The Christian sufferer need not know why the blow was struck. He wants to discover what God is doing in the face of it."

—AUSTIN FARRER

Gaining Insight

The child gingerly reaches her little hand up to the counter where the jar sits. "Sweetie, no cookies before dinner," says a voice from around the corner. The child swiftly pulls her hand down and thinks to herself, *How does Mom always know?* The phenomenon this child has stumbled upon has been called "mother's intuition"—a great tool God has given to women to anticipate children's behavior. But every person—male or female, parent or not—has access to an even greater form of intuition that can be called "godly, spiritual insight." Having insight about people or situations means that God has enabled us to see more than meets the eye. In turn, we are able to respond not just to the circumstances but to the unexpressed need. As we grow in our walk with Christ, so will our ability to see with spiritual eyes.

His **WORD:** Philippians 1:9–11

KNOWING *His* **HEART**

1. In verse 9, what is Paul's prayer for the church at Philippi?

2. What would be the result of this increased knowledge and depth of insight (verse 10)?

3. What does Paul say you will be filled with as your love increases (verse 11)?

4. What will be the ultimate purpose of love and righteousness (verse 11)?

KNOWING *My* HEART

1. What areas of your life could most benefit from increased knowledge and insight?

2. How could you gain more discernment for a current situation?

3. What do you think are some of the fruits of righteousness?

4. What can you do to fill your life with these fruits?

My HEART IN *His* HANDS

"I have more insight than all my teachers, for I meditate on your statutes."

—PSALM 119:99

Taking Action

The mark of a godly Christian is the ability to discern God's will and then to act upon it. Some of God's will is made very clear in His Word. For example, we know that stealing is never in God's will because one of the Ten Commandments says, "Do not steal." We also know that we have a responsibility to love people we don't like because God says, "Love your enemies." None of us have to question these areas of God's will. We just obey them. But other areas are more difficult to discern. They require following carefully in God's footsteps and listening to His Spirit. Discerning God's will also requires being willing to change our plans to do what God wants us to do. Both Deborah and Henrietta displayed characteristics of a woman who understood and followed God's will throughout her life.

His WORD: Judges 4:8–24

KNOWING *His* HEART

1. How was Deborah willing to change her plans to accomplish God's will (verses 8 and 9)?

2. What did Deborah say that shows she was hearing from God (verses 9 and 14)?

3. In what areas did Henrietta Mears especially need to listen to God and know His will?

4. What resulted from her willingness to adjust her life to follow God?

KNOWING *My* HEART

1. What evidences can you see of God directing your life in the past?

2. What areas are the most difficult for you to give over to God's control?

3. What steps can you take to more clearly discern God's will in a difficult area of your life?

4. What principles of godly behavior can you glean from an older friend?

My HEART IN *His* HANDS

"Every act should be performed as though all eternity depended on it."
— FRANZ ROSENWEIG

PART 4

Wisdom Is a Lifestyle

Perhaps you've heard stories about stupid antics of criminals. For instance, a bank robber handed the teller a note demanding money—and he had signed his name at the bottom! A group of thieves robbing a convenience store tore down the security camera and ripped up the video tape. But they neglected to disable a second security camera in another corner, which was humming along recording their faces as they tore up the first camera!

We laugh at those, but we find our own mistakes less humorous. They're painful! Some missteps we can't avoid because we're human and fallible. But many others we can sidestep by walking with our Lord Jesus Christ. He is our assurance that we can dodge the consequences of sin and spiritual immaturity.

In addition to growing beyond our childish mistakes, we have the privilege of challenging ourselves to go beyond our limitations. Both Deborah and Henrietta accepted challenges to act in situations they had never encountered before. Deborah was "a mother in Israel" when God called her to lead the nation. She judged cases that took a great deal of wisdom to settle, and even went out to war when the situation required. Surely, that was outside her comfort zone!

Henrietta was also a risk-taker in the name of the Lord. Tremendously handicapped by poor eyesight, she grew up with a godly mother and a visionary father. She had a heart to be used by God and believed Him for big ideas. God gave her wisdom and the ability to impart to others her vision for reaching the world, even in one of the world's most sophisticated places—Hollywood!

The good news is that God's wisdom is not just meted out to the rich and famous. In fact, the Lord honors the humble—no matter what their life circumstances are. We can have access to the Wisdom of the universe from our kitchen table, our office desk, or a Sunday school classroom.

What are some practical steps for gaining God's wisdom? Four stand out: trust God; fear God; study God's Word; ask God. The foundation of wisdom is a dynamic relationship with God.

If you had a teacher when you were young who encouraged your excitement in a certain subject, you can begin to grasp the thrill of persistently applying these four steps.

Take the challenge. As you grow in God's wisdom, your life will be more joyful. Dare to expand your horizons. As Miss Mears challenged in her last public message, "Just believe God." You'll never regret a moment of trusting your heart to the God of wisdom!

LESSON 16

Trust God

A long, metal tube hurtles through the air at hundreds of miles per hour, five to six miles up in the sky. Hundreds of people are crammed into this tube to travel long distances in the fastest time possible. The lives of these people are in the hands of a few strangers—the people guiding and controlling the long, metal tube. If you stop to think about it, the whole concept of commercial jetliners seems a little unbelievable. How many of us understand the aerodynamic principles that keep these tubes in the air? Yet we trust that the planes will fly where they are supposed to fly. How many of us know the men and women controlling the tubes—their beliefs, their intelligence, their competence? Yet we trust that because they are in the cockpit, they are qualified to be in control of the plane to get us safely to our destination. As we learn more about God, how much more should we trust in His control of our lives?

His **WORD:** Proverbs 3:5–8

KNOWING *His* HEART

1. What wise words are given regarding how we should think about our circumstances?

2. What should our actions demonstrate?

3. What promise does God give in verse 6?

4. What are we to do instead of looking to our own wisdom (verse 7)?

KNOWING *My* HEART

1. Think of the person you trust most. How do his or her qualities compare with God's qualities?

2. Describe the last significant challenge you have faced. How has your trust in God helped you through it?

3. What are some ways that you can acknowledge God in the activities of your day?

4. How will these wise words of Scripture help you determine God's path for your life?

My HEART IN *His* HANDS

"O Almighty God, when our vision fails and our understanding is darkened, when the ways of life seem hard and brightness of life is gone, grant to us the wisdom that deepens faith and enlarges trust."

—HAROLD VINCENT MILLIGAN

Fear God

There are two sides to the word "fear" as it relates to God. The first side expresses dread and terror in anticipation of His displeasure. The second side shows awe, reverence, and obedience. Often, we view the word as one or the other, but the two sides work together to show a more complete picture of how we should relate to God. The fear of His displeasure at our actions inspires us to obedience. Our awe and reverence for His power fill us with dread at the thought of going against His laws. But fear, with its complexities, is only one part of our relationship with God. Another part is love. All that God does for us, He does out of concern for our best interests. He chastens those He loves. So our fear should be like that of a child for a father—a father who loves his children, but who will discipline them for their own good and who is full of forgiveness.

His **WORD:** Psalm 25:8–15

KNOWING *His* HEART

1. From verses 8 and 9, describe how our "good and upright" God helps us.

2. Why does God forgive our sins, no matter how great (verse 11)?

3. What are the results for those who fear the Lord, as given in verses 12–14?

4. Why should we keep our eyes on the Lord?

KNOWING *My* HEART

1. How would you describe the "fear of the Lord"?

2. What would it mean for your life to have the Lord confide in you?

3. Describe a time when you heard from God as He guided you.

4. How can keeping your eyes on the Lord help you with a current struggle?

My HEART IN *His* HANDS

"When men no longer fear God, they transgress His Laws without hesitation."
—A. W. TOZER

LESSON 18

Study God's Word

Our lives are filled with books. As children, we had colorful storybooks read to us. Now, we gain knowledge and lose ourselves in fantastical fiction worlds. Regardless of our field of interest, the centerpiece of knowledge is a book. Is it any wonder that God chose the written word to reveal His will to mankind? The Bible is unlike any other book. God's Word has the power of His Spirit as its foundation. Hebrews 4:12 says, "The word of God is living and active. Sharper than any double-edged sword, it penetrates even to dividing soul and spirit, joints and marrow; it judges the thoughts and attitudes of the heart." We have no better tool for becoming all God wants us to be than learning and understanding the words from the Spirit of the Living God.

His **WORD:** Proverbs 2:1–10

KNOWING *His* HEART

1. What must we do to understand the fear of the Lord and find knowledge of God (verses 1–4)?

2. Besides wisdom, what else does the Lord give to us?

3. According to verses 7 and 8, what does God do for us?

4. How do verses 9 and 10 summarize the ultimate benefit of God's wisdom?

KNOWING *My* HEART

1. What does this passage say about the importance of God's Word in attaining wisdom?

2. Describe your devotional routine. How often do you study the Bible? Do you use a supplemental book? Do you have a special location where you study?

3. Based on this passage, what can you do to make God's Word a more integral part of your daily life?

4. As a child of God, what hope can you gain from verses 7 and 8?

My HEART IN *His* HANDS

"The Word of God offers to deliver more than we can ever possibly apply in one lifetime."

—JOSH MCDOWELL

LESSON 19

Ask God

Do you find it difficult to ask people for something you need or for help with a task? We may think, *They'll say no, so why bother asking?* When we make assumptions about how someone will respond, we may cheat ourselves out of receiving a blessing and cheat the other person out of being a blessing. But God wants us to ask Him for whatever we need. He wants to meet our needs and fulfill the desires of our hearts. He is waiting patiently for us to ask Him. God is not a "genie in a bottle" who will grant our every wish; instead, He is a loving heavenly Father who knows us better than we know ourselves. He will not only listen to our petitions, but He will answer them in our very best interest.

His **WORD:** James 1:5; Ephesians 1:17;
Psalm 119:26,27,66,73,125,135,144,169

KNOWING *His* **HEART**

1. What do the ten verses above have in common?

2. What do James 1:5 and Ephesians 1:17 say about wisdom?

3. In Psalm 119:26,27,66, the psalmist asks to be taught by God.

What does he want to be taught?

4. Referring to Psalm 119:73,125,135,144,169, list what the psalmist would like from God.

KNOWING *My* **HEART**

1. How has talking with God given you wisdom in your ministry? Your emotional needs? Your relationships with others?

2. God can give us wisdom, revelation, discernment, knowledge, good judgment, and understanding. Which would be the most valuable to you right now?

3. How does it give you hope for your future knowing that God wants to hear about your needs?

4. List two or three requests you have for God regarding needs in your life. Make these requests in your daily devotional time.

My **HEART IN** *His* **HANDS**

"*Prayer is designed more to adjust you to God than to adjust God to you.*"

—HENRY T. BLACKABY & CLAUDE V. KING

LESSON 20

Grow in Wisdom

Henrietta Mears' experience in secular education helped create a lifelong concern for better Christian education. At Hollywood Presbyterian Church, she realized the material they were using was grossly inadequate. There was no long-range plan for organizing lessons nor any relevance to age groups. So she began writing her own curriculum, pioneering age-grade materials. She printed the lessons on mimeograph machines and pasted pictures on the covers. Even so, her materials were the best available at that time. She learned more about teaching and writing material as she earnestly depended upon the Lord for wisdom. The Lord helped her grow in all aspects of her directorship as she tried to make the classroom learning environment better in every way—from painting classrooms to developing a mentoring relationship with her students.

His **WORD:** Luke 2:52; Ephesians 4:14–16

KNOWING *His* **HEART**

1. What example has Jesus given us in Luke 2:52?

2. What does this example mean for our lives?

3. How does Ephesians 4:14–16 describe this growth in wisdom?

4. Name two ways Henrietta Mears demonstrated the principles of Ephesians 4:14–16.

KNOWING *My* HEART

1. Consider your Christian growth over the past few years. In what ways have you gained wisdom?

2. How is Christ an example in the areas in which God is challenging you to grow?

3. How are you participating in the growth of another person? In the spiritual life of your church?

4. Considering Miss Mears' example, what do you expect God to do in your life to enable you to grow in ministry to others?

My HEART IN *His* HANDS

"Christ not only taught men, but he lived with them and guided them in every action."
—HENRIETTA MEARS

$\mathscr{D}$iscussion $\mathscr{G}$uide

If you are using *A Wise Heart* as a group study, the following answers to questions will help the facilitator guide the discussion. If you are studying the lessons on your own, refer to the answers after you have finished the lesson.

Answers are given for the first section of questions, called "Knowing His Heart." These questions are objective searches through the lesson's Bible passage. The second section, "Knowing My Heart," contains personal application questions to help you use the Bible truths in your daily life. Therefore, the answers will be unique to your situation.

If you are leading a group, discuss the first section more thoroughly, then allow volunteers to answer questions in the second section. Some answers may be so personal that group members will not want to express them aloud. Be sensitive to their feelings in this area.

The Lord bless you as you apply the steps to wisdom in your life!

Part 1: Wisdom Is a Choice

LESSON 1: I WANT TO BE WISE

1. Wisdom is shown by a good life, through deeds done in humility.

2. We are to refrain from boasting about these things or denying the truth that these attitudes are sinful.

3. The "wisdom" that comes from envy and selfish ambition is earthly, unspiritual, of the devil, and leads to disorder and

every evil practice.

4. Heavenly wisdom is pure, peace-loving, considerate, submissive, full of mercy and good fruit, impartial, sincere, and reaps a harvest of righteousness.

LESSON 2: I WANT TO MAKE WISE CHOICES

1. The foolish virgins took their lamps but no oil for the lamps to burn. The wise ones took their lamps and jars of oil.

2. All the virgins woke up and trimmed their lamps. The foolish ones asked to borrow oil from the wise ones, but the wise ones declined, saying there might not be enough oil. They told the foolish ones to go buy some oil.

3. They were ready for the bridegroom because they had oil in their lamps.

4. He refused to allow them in.

LESSON 3: WISDOM CAN BE SHARED

1. Pay attention, listen, apply our heart to them, keep them in our heart, be ready to share them.

2. So that our trust may be in the Lord.

3. They provide counsel and knowledge, and are true and reliable.

4. We should give accurate answers to others.

LESSON 4: THE RAIN WILL COME

1. A person who hears and practices God's Word is like a wise person who builds his house on a rock.

2. It is able to withstand rain, floods, and wind; it doesn't fall because of its secure foundation.

3. Someone who hears God's Word but does not put it into

practice is like a foolish person who builds his house on the sand.

4. It was unable to stand up under the rain, floods, and wind; it fell because it lacked the proper foundation.

LESSON 5: GOD HAS BIG PLANS

1. Israel had been cruelly oppressed for twenty years because they had sinned against God.

2. She was the leader of Israel and a prophetess of God. She had demonstrated that she had wisdom from God.

3. When Miss Mears was deciding whether to move to California, God gave her direction through a small, but clear, event—the selling of her house.

4. She shared through teaching, leadership, and creative productions of Bible study materials.

Part 2: Wisdom Leads Us to God

LESSON 6: GOD, THE ALL-POWERFUL

1. Wisdom and power.

2. He gives wisdom to the wise and knowledge to the discerning.

3. He changes times and seasons. He sets up and deposes kings.

4. He reveals what is deep and hidden and knows what lies in darkness.

LESSON 7: JESUS, OUR WISDOM

1. Not many were wise by human standards, influential, or of noble birth.

2. He chose the world's foolish and weak things to shame the

wise and strong. He chose the lowly and despised things, so that no one would boast before Him.

3. It comes from Christ Jesus, who has become for us wisdom from God.

4. Because Christ has made us what we are. He redeemed us and made us righteous and holy.

LESSON 8: GOD, OUR CREATOR

1. He is profoundly wise and vastly powerful.

2. The mountains are moved and overturned; the earth is shaken; the sun and stars are darkened.

3. He created the heavens and the seas. He precisely placed the stars to create the constellations.

4. With His power to perform wonders and innumerable miracles, He can surely meet our needs.

LESSON 9: THE HOLY SPIRIT, OUR GUIDE

1. A secret, hidden wisdom that God destined for our glory.

2. God has prepared more than we can imagine for those who love Him, and it has been revealed to us by His Spirit.

3. Just as only a man's spirit knows his own thoughts, so God's Spirit is the only One who knows God's thoughts.

4. We can understand what God has freely given us. We will speak with words taught by the Spirit, expressing spiritual truths with spiritual words. We will make judgments about all things, but we are not subject to any man's judgments. We have the mind of Christ.

LESSON 10: WISDOM'S RESULT, PEACE

1. God is praised by the offering of yourself to Him, by singing,

and by making music to the Lord.

2. The earth shook, the heavens poured, and the mountains quaked.

3. Many were willing to follow the Lord into battle. They recited the righteous acts of the Lord. They were thankful and jubilant.

4. Wisdom helps us know God's will for our life, and being in the center of God's will fills us with peace and joy.

Part 3: Wisdom Involves Action

LESSON 11: KNOWING GOD'S WILL

1. Be careful not to live as unwise, but as wise.

2. Living wisely helps us to make the most of every opportunity.

3. Because we are surrounded by evil in the world, we need to use our time wisely so we avoid temptation.

4. By understanding what the Lord's will is and being filled with the Holy Spirit.

LESSON 12: HAVING DISCERNMENT

1. Since both women claimed the child was hers, he ordered that the child be cut in two, and half be given to each woman.

2. The mother of the child pleaded with the king not to kill the child, but to give it to the other woman. The other woman said to cut the child in half so that neither woman would have him.

3. He ordered the child to be given to the first woman because he knew a loving mother would rather give up her child than

see the child killed. The woman who would just as soon see the child killed could not be the mother and would be likely to practice this deceit.

4. They were awed because they saw that he had wisdom from God.

LESSON 13: UNDERSTANDING GOD'S MYSTERY

1. To serve the Church by presenting the entire word of God.

2. It's described as a mystery that God did not reveal to earlier generations but that He now discloses to the Church.

3. Christ living in the believer, giving the hope of glory.

4. To proclaim Christ, to admonish and teach everyone with all wisdom, to present everyone perfect in Christ.

LESSON 14: GAINING INSIGHT

1. That their love may abound more and more in knowledge and depth of insight.

2. The ability to discern what is best and to be pure and blameless until Christ comes again.

3. The fruit of righteousness that comes from Jesus.

4. The glory and praise of God.

LESSON 15: TAKING ACTION

1. When Barak refused to face Sisera's army on his own, Deborah went with him.

2. She prophesied that a woman would defeat Sisera, and told Barak precisely when God would give Israel victory.

3. When she took a sabbatical from teaching; when she was offered a position at a church in California; when she wrote

Sunday school material.

4. She touched many lives for Christ. She influenced future leaders. Innumerable people have been discipled through her Bible study materials and the publishing house she founded.

Part 4: Wisdom Is a Lifestyle

LESSON 16: TRUST GOD

1. We should not rely on our own (limited and erroneous) understanding.

2. All of our actions should acknowledge the Lord by their merits.

3. When we acknowledge Him in all we do, He will make our paths straight.

4. We are to fear (revere) the Lord and turn from evil.

LESSON 17: FEAR GOD

1. He instructs sinners in His ways. He guides the humble in what is right, and He teaches them His way.

2. He forgives for the sake of His name.

3. We will receive God's instruction on the path for our life. We will prosper. And God will confide in us, making His covenant known to us.

4. Only He can release us from the sins that trap us.

LESSON 18: STUDY GOD'S WORD

1. Accept God's words, store up His commands within you, turn your ear to wisdom, apply your heart to understanding, call

out for insight, cry aloud for understanding, search for understanding as for silver or hidden treasure.

2. Knowledge and understanding.

3. He provides victory and protection and guards our way.

4. We will understand what is right, just, and fair; we will know the good paths to take; we will have wisdom.

LESSON 19: ASK GOD

1. They all contain a petition to God for various types of wisdom.

2. We should ask God for wisdom for ourselves and others, and He will give it generously so we can know Him better.

3. God's decrees, precepts, knowledge, and good judgment.

4. Understanding of God's commands, statutes, and decrees; understanding for life and of His Word.

LESSON 20: GROW IN WISDOM

1. In His humanity, He continued to grow and mature to be wise and favored by both God and people.

2. We need to keep growing in every way to be wiser in our walk with God and in relationships with others.

3. We will not be swayed by worldly teaching. We will speak the truth in love. We will become more like our Head, Christ, and will do our part in the body of Christ.

4. She was solid in her biblical foundation. She helped to build up others in the Body.

Beginning Your Journey of Joy

These four principles are essential in beginning a journey of joy.

One—God loves you and created you to know Him personally.

God's Love

"God so loved the world that He gave His one and only Son, that whoever believes in Him shall not perish but have eternal life" (John 3:16).

God's Plan

"Now this is eternal life: that they may know you, the only true God, and Jesus Christ, whom you have sent" (John 17:3).

What prevents us from knowing God personally?

Two—People are sinful and separated from God, so we cannot know Him personally or experience His love.

People are Sinful

"All have sinned and fall short of the glory of God" (Romans 3:23).

People were created to have fellowship with God; but, because of our own stubborn self-will, we chose to go our own independent way and fellowship with God was broken. This self-will, characterized by an attitude of active rebellion or passive indifference, is an evidence of what the Bible calls sin.

People are Separated

"The wages of sin is death" [spiritual separation from God] (Romans 6:23).

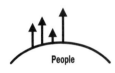

This diagram illustrates that God is holy and people are sinful. A great gulf separates the two. The arrows illustrate that people are continually trying to reach God and establish a personal relationship with Him through our own efforts, such as a good life, philosophy, or religion—but we inevitably fail.

The third principle explains the only way to bridge this gulf...

Three—*Jesus Christ is God's only provision for our sin. Through Him alone we can know God personally and experience His love.*

He Died In Our Place

"God demonstrates His own love toward us, in that while we were yet sinners, Christ died for us" (Romans 5:8).

He Rose from the Dead

"Christ died for our sins...He was buried...He was raised on the third day according to the Scriptures...He appeared to Peter, then to the twelve. After that He appeared to more than five hundred..." (1 Corinthians 15:3–6).

He Is the Only Way to God

"Jesus said to him, 'I am the way, and the truth, and the life; no one comes to the Father but through Me'" (John 14:6).

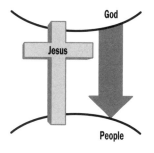

This diagram illustrates that God has bridged the gulf that separates us from Him by sending His Son, Jesus Christ, to die on the cross in our place to pay the penalty for our sins.

It is not enough just to know these three truths...

Four—We must individually receive Jesus Christ as Savior and Lord; then we can know God personally and experience His love.

We Must Receive Christ

"As many as received Him, to them He gave the right to become children of God, even to those who believe in His name" (John 1:12).

We Receive Christ Through Faith

"By grace you have been saved through faith; and that not of yourselves, it is the gift of God; not as a result of works that no one should boast" (Ephesians 2:8,9).

When We Receive Christ, We Experience a New Birth
(Read John 3:1–8.)

We Receive Christ By Personal Invitation

[Christ speaking] "Behold, I stand at the door and knock; if any-one hears My voice and opens the door, I will come in to him" (Revelation 3:20).

Receiving Christ involves turning to God from self (repentance) and trusting Christ to come into our lives to forgive us of our sins and to make us what He wants us to be. Just to agree intellectu-ally that Jesus Christ is the Son of God and that He died on the cross for our sins is not enough. Nor is it enough to have an emotional experience. We receive Jesus Christ by faith, as an act of our will.

These two circles represent two kinds of lives:

Self-Directed Life
S – Self is on the throne
✝ – Christ is outside the life
● – Interests are directed by self, often resulting in discord and frustration

Christ-Directed Life
✝ – Christ is in the life and on the throne
S – Self is yielding to Christ
● – Interests are directed by Christ, resulting in harmony with God's plan

Which circle best represents your life?
Which circle would you like to have represent your life?

The following explains how you can receive Christ:

You Can Receive Christ Right Now by Faith Through Prayer
(Prayer is talking with God)

God knows your heart and is not so concerned with your words as He is with the attitude of your heart. The following is a suggested prayer:

> *Lord Jesus, I want to know You personally. Thank You for dying on the cross for my sins. I open the door of my life and receive You as my Savior and Lord. Thank You for forgiving my sins and giving me eternal life. Take control of the throne of my life. Make me the kind of person You want me to be.*

Does this prayer express the desire of your heart?

If it does, I invite you to pray this prayer right now, and Christ will come into your life, as He promised.

How to Know That Christ Is in Your Life

Did you receive Christ into your life? According to His promise in Revelation 3:20, where is Christ right now in relation to you?

Christ said that He would come into your life. Would He mislead you? On what authority do you know that God has answered your prayer? (The trustworthiness of God Himself and His Word.)

The Bible Promises Eternal Life to All Who Receive Christ

"The witness is this, that God has given us eternal life, and this life is in His Son. He who has the Son has the life; he who does not have the Son of God does not have the life. These things I have written to you who believe in the name of the Son of God, in order that you may know that you have eternal life" (1 John 5:11–13).

Thank God often that Christ is in your life and that He will never leave you (Hebrews 13:5). You can know on the basis of His promise that Christ lives in you and that you have eternal life from the very moment you invite Him in. He will not deceive you.

An important reminder...

Feelings Can Be Unreliable

You might have expectations about how you should feel after placing your trust in Christ. While feelings are important, they are unreliable indicators of your sincerity or the trustworthiness of God's promise. Our feelings change easily, but God's Word and His character remain constant. This illustration shows the relationship among **fact** (God and His Word), **faith** (our trust in God and His Word), and our **feelings**.

Fact: The chair is strong enough to support you.

Faith: You believe this chair will support you, so you sit in it.

Feeling: You may or may not feel comfortable in this chair, but it continues to support you.

The promise of God's Word, the Bible—not our feelings—is our authority. The Christian lives by faith (trust) in the trustworthiness of God Himself and His Word.

Now That You Have Entered Into a Personal Relationship With Christ

The moment you received Christ by faith, as an act of your will, many things happened, including the following:

- Christ came into your life (Revelation 3:20; Colossians 1:27).

- Your sins were forgiven (Colossians 1:14).

- You became a child of God (John 1:12).

- You received eternal life (John 5:24).

- You began the great adventure for which God created you (John 10:10; 2 Corinthians 5:17; 1 Thessalonians 5:18).

Can you think of anything more wonderful that could happen to you than entering into a personal relationship with Jesus Christ? Would you like to thank God in prayer right now for what He has done for you? By thanking God, you demonstrate your faith.

To enjoy your new relationship with God...

Suggestions for Christian Growth

Spiritual growth results from trusting Jesus Christ. "The righteous man shall live by faith" (Galatians 3:11). A life of faith will enable you to trust God increasingly with every detail of your life, and to practice the following:

G *Go* to God in prayer daily (John 15:7).

R *Read* God's Word daily (Acts 17:11); begin with the Gospel of John.

O *Obey* God moment by moment (John 14:21).

W *Witness* for Christ by your life and words (Matthew 4:19; John 15:8).

T *Trust* God for every detail of your life (1 Peter 5:7).

H *Holy Spirit*—allow Him to control and empower your daily life and witness (Galatians 5:16,17; Acts 1:8; Ephesians 5:18).

Fellowship in a Good Church

God's Word admonishes us not to forsake "the assembling of ourselves together" (Hebrews 10:25). Several logs burn brightly together, but put one aside on the cold hearth and the fire goes out. So it is with your relationship with other Christians. If you do not belong to a church, do not wait to be invited. Take the initiative; call the pastor of a nearby church where Christ is honored and His Word is preached. Start this week, and make plans to attend regularly.

Resources

My Heart in His Hands: Devotional Series. Finding security does not happen by accident but by placing your heart in God's hands. Vonette Bright desires for women to experience God's forgiveness and discover the pure delight of living for Christ. Four devotional volumes containing brief inspirational readings focus on the practical aspects of the seasons of life God has designed. The readings conclude with suggested biblical passages and an appropriate response for each day.

Renew a Steadfast Spirit Within Me. Spring—renewal is everywhere; we are reminded to cry out to God, "Renew a steadfast spirit within me." The first of four books in Vonette Bright's devotional series, this book will give fresh spiritual vision and hope to women of all ages. ISBN 1-56399-161-6

Set Me Free Indeed. Summer—a time of freedom. Are there bonds that keep you from God's best? With this devotional, a few moments daily can help you draw closer to the One who gives true freedom. This is the second of four in the devotional series. ISBN 1-56399-162-4

I Delight Greatly in My Lord. Do you stop to appreciate the blessings God has given you? Spend time delighting in God with book three in this devotional series. ISBN 1-56399-163-2

Lead Me in the Way Everlasting. We all need guidance, and God is the ultimate leader. These daily moments with God will help you to rely on His leadership. The final in the four-book devotional series. ISBN 1-56399-164-0

My Heart in His Hands: Bible Study Guides. Designed to complement the topics of the four devotional books in this series, the Bible Study Guides allow a woman to examine God's Word and gain perspective on the issues that touch her life. Each study highlights a biblical character and includes an inspirational portrait of a woman who served God.

Available in 2002:
A Renewed Heart (1-56399-176-4)
A Nurturing Heart (1-56399-177-2)
A Woman's Heart (1-56399-178-0)
A Free Heart (1-56399-179-9)
A Wise Heart (1-56399-180-2)
A Caring Heart (1-56399-181-0)

Available in 2003:
A Willing Heart (1-56399-182-9)
A Simple Heart (1-56399-183-7)
A Joyful Heart (1-56399-184-5)
A Guided Heart (1-56399-185-3)
An Intimate Heart (1-56399-186-1)
A Growing Heart (1-56399-187-X)

The Joy of Hospitality: Fun Ideas for Evangelistic Entertaining. Co-written with Barbara Ball, this practical book tells how to share your faith through hosting barbecues, coffees, holiday parties, and other events in your home. ISBN 1-56399-057-1

The Joy of Hospitality Cookbook. Filled with uplifting scriptures and quotations, this cookbook contains hundreds of delicious recipes, hospitality tips, sample menus, and family traditions that are sure to make your entertaining a memorable and eternal success. Co-written with Barbara Ball. ISBN 1-56399-077-6

The Greatest Lesson I've Ever Learned. In this treasury of in-spiring, real-life experiences, twenty-three prominent women of faith share their "greatest lessons." Does God have faith- and character-building lessons for you in their rich, heart-warming stories? ISBN 1-56399-085-7

Beginning Your Journey of Joy. This adaptation of the *Four Spiritual Laws* speaks in the language of today's women and of-fers a slightly feminine approach to sharing God's love with your neighbors, friends, and family members. ISBN 1-56399-093-8

These and other fine products from *NewLife* Pub-lications are available from your favorite bookseller or by calling (800) 235-7255 (within U.S.) or (407) 826-2145, or by visiting www.newlifepubs.com.